Giant Leaps

The Apollo Moonwalkers

Stuart A. Kallen

ABDO & Daughters
PUBLISHING

Published by Abdo & Daughters, 4940 Viking Dr., Suite 622, Edina, MN 55435.

Cover Photos by: Archive Photos
Inside Photos
Archive Photos: pp. 4-5, 9, 13, 21, 22, 23, 27, 28
AP/Wide World Photos: pp. 7, 9, 15, 16, 19, 27
Bettmann: p. 11

Edited by Bob Italia

Library of Congress Cataloging–in–Publication Data
Kallen, Stuart A., 1955–
The Apollo moonwalkers / Stuart A. Kallen
    p. cm. — (Giant leaps)
Includes bibliographical references (p. 31) and index.
Summary: Tells the story of NASA's mission to put a man on the moon through Project Apollo which completed six moon landings between 1969 and 1972.
    ISBN 1-56239-566-1
    1. Project Apollo (U.S.)—Juvenile literature. [1. Project Apollo (U.S.)]
I. Title. II. Series.
    TL789.8.U6A5425 1996
    629.45'4—dc20
                                  95-40516
                                     CIP
                                     AC

CONTENTS

FLAMING CHARIOTS ACROSS THE SKY

I believe this nation should commit itself to achieving the goal, before the decade is out, of landing a man on the moon and returning him safely to earth. - President John F. Kennedy, May 25, 1961.

TO THE ANCIENT GREEKS, Apollo was the most important god. He was the god of youth and beauty. He was the god of poetry, music, and wisdom. And Apollo was the sun god who rode his flaming chariot across the sky. When the American government space agency, the National Aeronautics and Space Administration (NASA), needed a name for their mission to put a man on the moon, Apollo seemed like the right choice. Project Apollo was born. NASA promised the world that within nine years, an American would walk on the moon.

This page: Apollo 15 blasts off from Cape Canaveral.

By the time President Kennedy made his famous speech, the United States had already put a man in space. Alan Shepard was launched in the *Mercury 7* capsule into a sub-orbital flight on May 5, 1961. A rapid series of Project Mercury spaceflights taught scientists and astronauts valuable information they needed to go farther into space.

There was urgency in NASA's mission. They were competing with the Soviet Union, America's enemy at the time. The two powerful countries, called superpowers, were locked in a battle of ideas and strength. Each superpower flexed its muscle by building powerful rockets armed with nuclear warheads. The two nations had thousands of rockets pointed at each other. If a war was fought with these weapons, the world would be destroyed. With tensions high, this period, from 1945 to 1991, was called the Cold War.

THE MISSION OF APOLLO

Project Apollo's goal was to launch a spacecraft from earth's surface, which spins through space at 1,000 miles (1,609 kilometers) per hour. The spacecraft must go into earth's orbit at 18,000 miles (28,962 kilometers) per hour, then speed up to 25,000 miles (40,225 kilometers) per hour. The craft would then have to leave the pull of earth's gravity and travel to the moon, 240,000 miles (386,160 kilometers) away.

Once the spacecraft reached the moon, it would go into orbit. Then men had to drop down to the moon's surface in a special landing craft called a lunar module (LM). The astronauts would take scientific measurements, collect specimens, and leave instruments that would send information back to earth. Then they had to return to the LM, fly back to the spacecraft, and return to earth's orbit. Once in orbit around the earth, the spacecraft would fly back into the earth's atmosphere and drop by parachute into the ocean. This was not a simple operation.

Over 10,000 separate tasks needed to be accomplished for a lunar landing. The LM alone would have over one million parts packed into a craft the size of a delivery van. Dozens of unmanned flights would have to be launched to test equipment, map the surface of the moon, and confirm safety. Sending a living astronaut to the moon's surface was the last mission in a long series of lunar probes.

Landing an astronaut on the moon was the most complicated task ever taken up by human beings. The technology was unproved or did not exist. Small computers were years in the future. The rocket engines needed for a lunar landing were not invented yet. Space suits to protect the astronauts did not yet exist. But the finest minds in America pulled together with scientists from other countries. Project Apollo was getting ready to fly.

Right: A photo of the nearly full moon taken by *Apollo 8.*

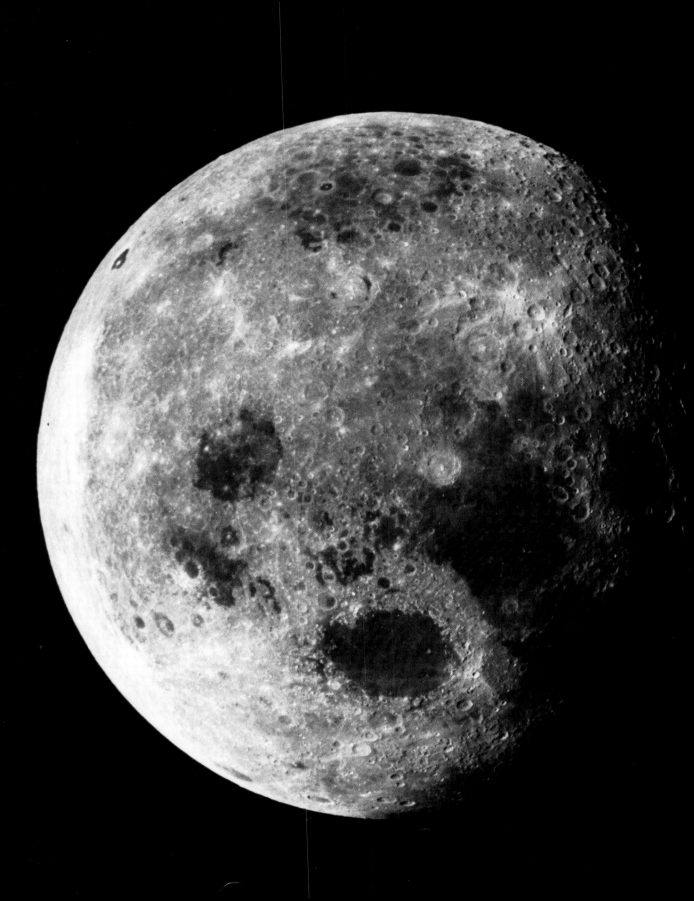

TRAGEDY

It was early afternoon on January 27, 1967, at the Kennedy Space Center in Florida. Astronauts Virgil I. (Gus) Grissom, Edward H. White, and Roger B. Chaffee put on their space suits and climbed into the *Apollo I* command module. The spacecraft was sitting on top of a 363-foot (112.5-meter) tall Saturn booster rocket. Technicians sealed the hatch behind the astronauts. Another long day of testing began. For every hour that a spacecraft spent in orbit, thousands of hours of flight rehearsals and system checks were performed.

Once again the astronauts went through the motions of a real launch while sitting quietly in the module. This would be Grissom's third spaceflight and White's second. At 6:31 p.m., Grissom yelled over the radio, "Fire! We've got a fire in the cockpit...We've got a bad fire...let's get out...open 'er up...we're burning up." These were the last words from the command module.

NASA technicians scrambled to open the hatch. They were driven back by heat and smoke. When they finally opened the hatch they saw a horrible scene. The module had been badly burned. Grissom, White, and Chaffee were dead.

The fire shocked NASA and America. It was discovered that a short in a wire caused a spark to ignite the pure oxygen that was used in the cockpit. (Pure oxygen is flammable. The air we breathe is made of oxygen and nitrogen.) Because of the sealed hatch, there was no escape for the astronauts.

Nineteen sixty-seven was a bad year for the Soviets as well. Little more than three months after the Apollo fire, the Soviets launched their version of Apollo, which was called *Soyuz I*.

After 17 orbits around the earth, Soyuz attempted reentry. But its parachute did not open. Soviet cosmonaut Vladimir Komarov was killed when *Soyuz I* hit the ground.

The two tragedies marked a turning point for both countries. The space race was over. The Soviets hoped their Soyuz program would challenge Apollo. But after the death of Komarov, the Soviets had

problems with their rocket boosters. They began to give up the idea of a lunar landing and began work on long-term, manned orbital operations, like space stations. It was important work that could be used to send people to Mars and beyond.

After the deaths of Gus Grissom, Ed White, and Roger Chaffee, NASA became more firm in its mission. The *Apollo 1* astronauts would not die in vain. Some day soon, an American would walk on the moon.

Above top, left to right: Gus Grissom, Edward White, Roger Chaffee.
Above: The charred interior of the *Apollo 1* space capsule.

APOLLO STRIKES BACK

After the fire, NASA's leaders worked hard to put Apollo back on track. They had three years to fulfill their promise to the American people of a manned lunar landing.

On November 9, 1967, NASA launched *Apollo 4*. It was an unmanned Saturn rocket that weighed over 3,000 tons (2,721 metric tons). It was the heaviest object to ever fly. Its five F-1 booster engines made it the world's most powerful machine. The rocket reached 25,000 miles (40,225 kilometers) per hour. The rocket's stages separated perfectly. The unmanned craft orbited flawlessly and splashed down in the Pacific Ocean carried by three parachutes. The system had worked. This was the rocket that would carry men to the moon.

The next manned mission was *Apollo 7,* flown by Navy Captain Walter M. Schirra, civilian test pilot Walter R. Cunningham, and Air Force Major Donn F. Eisele. It had been 20 months since an American

had been in space—the last flight of the Gemini program. The fire and several other equipment failures had grounded NASA.

On the morning of October 11, 1968, *Apollo 7* lifted off perfectly when its Saturn V rocket ignited. This was Schirra's third spaceflight. It was the first for the other astronauts. Their ride on the Saturn booster was bumpy for a few minutes. The ignition of the second stage felt like a swift kick in the back. After a short time, the crew was in orbit.

The flight's mission was to test the combined command and service module (CSM) that would carry astronauts *back* from the moon after a lunar landing. After a successful test of the CSM's engines, Schirra radioed back to NASA with the message: "Yabba-dabba-doo!"

The Apollo capsule was bigger than Mercury or Gemini. Like the other two, Apollo was shaped like an upside-down badminton "birdie." But it carried its three astronauts on collapsible couches near a large center hatch. When the center couch was stowed after liftoff, the crew had plenty of room to stretch or curl up. The spacecraft was equipped with guidance systems, communications gear, and computers that were far superior to Gemini or Mercury. When the cone-shaped command module was coupled to the service module, the craft looked like a blunt-nosed bullet.

Unfortunately, the module's windows fogged up from the astronaut's breathing. And the astronauts all caught bad colds. But their performance was perfect. Live TV coverage gave the entire world a view of life in space. For 10 days Schirra and the crew floated above the world. After splashdown in the Atlantic less than 1 mile (1.6 kilometers) from target, NASA called the mission "101 percent successful."

Right: The world's mightiest rocket—the giant Saturn V, noses into clouds of smoke as it lifts slowly from its launch pad.

APOLLO ORBITS THE MOON

On December 21, 1968, Colonel Frank Borman, Captain James A. Lovell, and Lieutenant Colonel William A. Anders readied for the flight of *Apollo 8*. The Saturn V rocket was filled with 2,000 tons (1,814 metric tons) of explosive propellant. At 7:51 a.m. the fiery rocket launched into space. Twelve minutes later *Apollo 8* was in orbit.

The rocket motor devoured 80 tons (72.6 metric tons) of supercold propellant. *Apollo 8* reached a speed of 23,226 miles (37,370 kilometers) per hour. The spacecraft traveled fast enough to escape the earth's gravity. And it was the fastest a human had ever traveled. "You're on your way!" yelled Mission Control. "You're *really* on your way!"

For the first time in history, the pull of earth's gravity was cut for a few men. The earth was 25,000 miles (40,225 kilometers) behind the astronauts. They were on their way to the moon. But the astronauts were spacesick—dizzy and nauseous. They tried to sleep.

The next morning the astronauts were 100,000 miles (160,900 kilometers) from earth. They sent back live TV pictures of the earth as it had never been seen before. It looked like "a warm blue sphere with huge covers of white clouds."

The men strapped themselves into their launch couches. Once they crossed behind the moon, they would be out of contact with Mission Control in Houston, Texas. For 40 minutes they would be on the dark side of the moon. Computers counted down the minutes and fired the rockets to launch the Apollo module into lunar orbit. Within moments, the astronauts unstrapped themselves and floated to the windows. They gazed in awe at the gray moonscape 70 miles (112 kilometers) below. On earth it was Christmas Eve.

As the day wore on, *Apollo 8* drifted slowly around the moon. Anders described it as "a very whitish gray, like dirty beach sand with lots of footprints in it." The "footprints" were craters. The astronauts photographed the surface for future moon landings. After an emotional Christmas celebration from cold, black space, the crew slept.

Apollo 8 circled the moon for 20 hours and 9 minutes—10 orbits. Now it was time to fire the rockets to return *Apollo 8* to earth. Lovell radioed to the nervous techs at Mission Control: "Houston, please be informed, there is a Santa Claus." The rockets had fired perfectly. The victorious astronauts were on their way home.

Below: An overall view of the Mission Operations Control Room in the Mission Control Center.

SURVEYOR AND RANGER

The *Apollo 8* mission had achieved all of its goals. And it had returned morale to NASA, badly needed after the *Apollo 1* fire. The next flight, *Apollo 9,* would be an earth orbit of the Lunar Module (LM). This vehicle would take the astronauts from the Apollo spacecraft and land them on the moon. Then it would bring them back—if everything worked right.

Work on an LM began in 1962. At the time, scientists did not know if the surface of the moon would hold a heavy spacecraft. Some thought the moon's surface might be dust that would swallow up the vehicle and the astronauts. Then again, the surface might be a crust, which would crack when the LM landed, pitching it on its side.

In 1964, NASA launched *Ranger 7,* a satellite that sent over 4,000 moon photographs back to earth. The pictures showed a heavily cratered surface. *Ranger 8* and *Ranger 9* sent back 13,000 pictures in 1965. Next,

NASA sent a Surveyor satellite to land on the moon, take soil tests, chemical analysis, and photographs. On February 3, 1966, *Surveyor I* landed on the moon. It weighed 594 pounds (269 kilograms). Surveyor sent back 11,000 photographs and showed that the surface of the moon could support a spacecraft. In fact, the moon looked like a freshly-plowed field. Four more Surveyors landed and showed the moon rock to be like volcanic rock on earth.

While Surveyor was doing its work, NASA launched five camera spacecraft to photograph the lunar surface. Soon they had a map of the moon. Apollo landing sights could be selected.

With that information, NASA refined the LM's design. The final model stood almost 23 feet (7 meters) high. It was held up by four spider-like legs that were folded up during flight. It weighed 33,000 pounds (14,965 kilograms).

The hardest part of Lunar Module design was the rocket engines. Until that time, rocket engines were designed to be either on or off. A soft moon landing would require the rockets to fire at higher or lower speeds. They needed to be throttled like a gas pedal regulates the speed of a car motor. New computer technology made this possible.

Below: A photo diagram showing the landing site of *Apollo 11* on the moon's Sea of Tranquility. The picture was taken during the flight of *Apollo 10.*

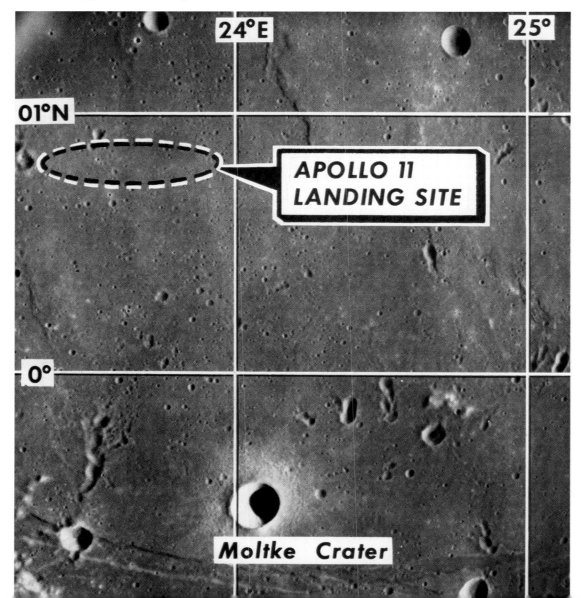

FIRST FLIGHT OF THE LM

Apollo 9 was flown by Colonel James A. McDivitt, Colonel David R. Scott, and Russell L. Schweickart. It was launched March 3, 1969, and stayed in orbit 10 days. The mission rehearsed rendezvous and docking procedures with the Lunar Module in earth orbit.

First they had to separate the LM from the command module. After the LM was free-floating in space, the astronauts turned around and docked with it—nose to nose. This was a tricky procedure that required great skill from the astronauts.

After docking, Jim McDivitt crawled through the tunnel between the command module and the LM. Schweickart followed. The men fought spacesickness as they prepared to take the LM on its first spaceflight. The 16-ton (14.5-metric ton) LM was a noisy vehicle with chattering fans and rumbling gongs.

The crew called the LM *Spider* because of its shape. They called the command module *Gumdrop* for the same reason. For three days the two linked craft orbited the earth. Then the astronauts put on their space suits. They prepared to fly the LM by itself. This was very dangerous because if the two craft could not re-dock, the astronauts in the LM could not return to earth.

Spider separated from *Gumdrop* as planned. The men in the module fired thruster rockets and flew through space on their own. Then *Spider* and *Gumdrop* successfully re-docked. Once again, cheers went up at Mission Control. We were one step closer to the moon.

Below: The *Apollo 9* Lunar Module flying high above earth.

THE LM ORBITS THE MOON

On May 18, 1969, *Apollo 10* lifted off. Colonel Thomas P. Stafford, Navy Commander Eugene A. Cernan, and Commander John W. Young were going to orbit the moon. Stafford and Cernan would fly the LM within 10 miles (16 kilometers) of the lunar surface.

On liftoff the rockets shook violently as the stages separated. The crew was slammed back and forth. The astronauts were alarmed the vibrations would damage the LM.

Once *Apollo 10* was in orbit they found that nothing had been damaged. Two and a half hours after liftoff, the computers fired the boosters and *Apollo 10* reached earth escape velocity—25,000 miles (40,150 kilometers) per hour.

For two days the earth became smaller and smaller. This time the crew was spared the spacesickness that had affected the others. Soon the crew was in orbit 75 miles (120 kilometers) above the moon.

With little effort, Stafford and Cernan suited up and crawled into the LM. The computers fired the rockets and within 57 minutes they were circling the moon. The crew inspected the Sea of Tranquility and found a perfect landing site for the next Apollo mission. They turned around and headed back.

Suddenly the LM threw itself into a violent spin. For several seconds the men yelled commands back and forth. Stafford took the controls away from the computer and flew the LM manually. Somehow someone had accidentally thrown a wrong computer switch. This fired a rocket engine that should have been off. When the computer was switched off, things returned to normal. Badly shaken, the astronauts safely docked the LM with the command module.

The whole operation took less than eight hours. Stafford and Cernan had flown within 47,000 feet (14,579 meters) of the moon's surface. The *Apollo 10* splashed down on May 26. President Kennedy's dream of landing a man on the moon was one step closer to reality.

ONE GIANT LEAP FOR MANKIND

During the weeks before the *Apollo 11* moonlanding, astronauts Neil Armstrong, Colonel Edward E. (Buzz) Aldrin, and Michael Collins trained endlessly. They put on their hot space suits and rehearsed moon walking in a crushed lava rock "sandbox." They practiced in a LM simulator just like the one that would land on the moon. A television camera projected images of a moonlanding on the module's windows.

Meanwhile, the Soviet Union was preparing for its own moonlanding. They knew the Americans would beat them. But they were hoping to put a cosmonaut on the moon soon after the Americans. On July 4, 1969, the Soviets tried to launch an unmanned lunar module. Something went wrong and the rocket exploded on the launch pad. No one was killed, but the Soviets were set back in their quest to walk on the moon.

On July 16, 1969, over one million people gathered on the beaches around Cape Canaveral. They had come to watch the launch of *Apollo 11*. There were campfires on the beaches, tents and campers along the roads, thousands of boats on the sea, and over 200,000 cars clogging the highways. Millions more watched the event on television.

The Saturn V rocket sat on the launch pad. It had the explosive power of an atomic bomb. Over one million separate parts were contained in the command, service, and lunar modules, which weighed over 50 tons (45 metric tons). The command module was called the *Columbia*. The LM was called *Eagle*.

At 9:32 a.m., *Apollo 11* lifted off. Within hours the astronauts escaped earth's gravity and were on their way to the moon. After a quick TV tour of the module, the crew bedded down to sleep. Three air-breathing creatures went to bed in a little bubble of oxygen floating through the

Right: A Saturn V rocket rollout from the vertical assembly building to the launch pad.

vacuum of space. Their spacecraft was a miniature planet. They lived inside, separated from death by an inch or two of metal and plastic.

After two full days of space travel, the men were 150,000 miles (241,359 kilometers) from earth. The moon was 30 hours away. Neil Armstrong began thinking about what he would say when he stepped onto the moon. Armstrong and Aldrin pulled themselves into the *Eagle* and began an endless series of equipment checks.

On July 20, *Apollo 11* was in orbit around the moon. Mission Control signalled the spacecraft with, "You are go for separation."

"The *Eagle* has wings," Armstrong called back as the LM separated from *Columbia*. Within 12 minutes, the astronauts would land on the moon.

As the *Eagle* began its final descent on the moon, the onboard computer flashed a coded signal that meant "overload." It threw a scare into everyone back at Mission Control. But the computer experts suspected that the problem wasn't serious. They gave the go-ahead for the astronauts to land.

The ground below the *Eagle* looked bad. With the computer scare, the astronauts didn't have time to search for a landing spot. The computer was taking them toward a huge crater surrounded by boulders. Armstrong took control from the computer. He slowed the *Eagle* as the module skimmed forward. The low-fuel light began to blink. They had 60 seconds of fuel left to land. If they ran out of fuel, they would crash into the surface of the moon.

With 30 seconds left, the *Eagle* was 30 feet (9 meters) above the moon's surface. The plumes of the module's engines disturbed the dust that had lain still for one billion years. The men inside the LM were busy reading out the landing checklist: "Mode controls, both auto, descent engine command override, off. Engine arm off." Armstrong stared out at the bleak surface of the moon. He spoke: "Houston? Tranquility Base here. The *Eagle* has landed."

Mission Control answered: "Roger, Tranquility. We [hear] you on the ground. You've got a bunch of guys about to turn blue here. We're breathing again. Thanks a lot."

Right: Astronaut Buzz Aldrin steps out onto the lunar surface.

After describing the look of the moon to the world, the astronauts ate dinner. Then they suited up for their moonwalk, which took several hours. On earth, the space suit and breathing pack weighed 190 pounds (86 kilograms). In the light gravity of the moon it weighed 30 pounds (13 kilograms). With their space suits on, each astronaut weighed about 60 pounds (26 kilograms).

Seven hours after landing on the moon, the men opened the *Eagle's* hatch. Armstrong moved carefully down the ladder, then stepped onto the moon. Next he spoke the words: "That's one small step for man, one giant leap for mankind."

Soon Aldrin was out of the LM

Below: Buzz Aldrin placing the American flag on the moon.

hopping around in the light moon gravity. There was no atmosphere to reflect light as on earth. The sun threw a harsh searchlight over everything. Shadows were pure black. Pebbles, rocks, and craters covered the surface. "Isn't that something?" said Armstrong. "Magnificent sight out here."

"Beautiful, beautiful," said Aldrin.

The men unveiled a plaque that they had brought from earth. It read: "Here men from the planet earth first set foot upon the moon. July, 1969 A.D. We came in peace for all mankind."

The moonwalking astronauts performed a series of scientific experiments. They gathered soil from the lunar surface. As the largest TV audience in history watched, Aldrin planted the American flag on the moon's surface. It was held aloft by an aluminum bar, since there is no wind on the moon. One billion TV watchers— more than 25% of all the people on earth—watched the two astronauts salute the flag.

President Richard Nixon spoke to the astronauts. "For one priceless moment, in the whole history of man, all the people on earth are truly one."

With minutes left in their mission, Aldrin took a small packet from his space suit. It contained the shoulder patches from the tragic *Apollo 1* mission along with two medals from Soviet cosmonauts who had died. Aldrin also had a small gold olive branch that stood for peace. Included in the packet was a small silicon disk that had goodwill messages from 73 nations, including the Soviet Union. It read, "From the Planet Earth." Aldrin tossed the package of peace offerings into the moon's soil and climbed back aboard the *Eagle*.

The astronauts stowed 40 pounds (18 kilograms) of moon rocks in the LM. They threw their unneeded equipment onto the moon's surface. They had gritty moon dust smeared on their clothing. The astronauts ate and tried to sleep, but couldn't.

Seven hours later, the *Eagle* lifted off from the moon. Four hours after leaving the Sea of Tranquility, the *Columbia* and the *Eagle* were docked. The astronauts hadn't slept in 40 hours. They said goodbye to the moon and crawled back into the command module. Within days, the Apollo moonwalkers splashed down safely on earth.

When the astronauts landed, they had to be kept separate from other people. No one knew if a strange germ existed on the moon which might wipe out the human race. This separation was called a quarantine.

The first quarantine quarters were a modified aluminum house trailer on the deck of the recovery ship *Hornet*. President Nixon officially welcomed the weary moon travelers back to earth through the trailer's window. Twenty days later the astronauts were released from quarantine, since they hadn't become sick. On August 13, the three men rode down Broadway in New York City. The streets boomed with cheers and applause. The air was full of confetti and ticker tape. It was a triumphant celebration of American bravery and know-how.

Below: President Richard Nixon talking to the *Apollo 11* astronauts while in quarantine.

UNLUCKY 13

After the success of *Apollo 11* the race to the moon ended. The Soviet Union announced they would no longer attempt a moon landing but would concentrate on manned flights in earth orbit.

With *Apollo 12* the U.S. began more intense scientific investigations of the moon. Navy Commanders Charles (Pete) Conrad, Jr. and Alan L. Bean landed the LM *Intrepid* on the moon on November 18, 1969 in an area called the Ocean of Storms. Commander Richard F. Gordon cruised overhead in lunar orbit in the command module *Yankee Clipper.* Conrad and Bean made two separate moonwalks. They set up many instruments that had been designed for an Apollo Lunar Scientific Experiments Package (ALSEP). The instruments read moonquakes, magnetic fields, solar wind particles, and surface gases. The instruments radioed information back to earth for years after the astronauts had safely returned home.

The people at NASA are not the types to believe a number could bring bad luck. But there were a lot of 13's in NASA's next moon mission.

Apollo 13 was scheduled for liftoff at 13:13 Houston time (1:13 p.m.). The spacecraft would enter the moon's orbit on April 13.

But the problems of *Apollo 13* were not the fault of unlucky numbers. There were other bad omens as well. First, command module pilot Thomas (Ken) Mattingly was pulled from the flight two days before launch. He had been exposed to German measles and NASA doctors did not want him to get sick in outer space. But Mattingly had trained with *Apollo 13's* other crew members—James Lovell and Fred W. Haise, Jr.—for two years. Mattingly was replaced by John L. Swigert, who had only trained with the crew for two days.

Another problem was an oxygen tank that did not work properly. The tank had been pulled from the *Apollo 10* spacecraft and was supposed to be fixed. But NASA technicians spent several days trying to get the tank to work right for *Apollo 13*. They thought they had it fixed—but they were wrong.

After *Apollo 13* blasted off on April 10, 1970, one of the engines shut down two minutes early. This was a minor problem but another bad sign. Two days into the flight—on April 13—*Apollo 13* looked like the smoothest flight of the space program. The crew sent a 49-minute live-TV broadcast back to earth showing people how the astronauts worked and lived in space. But America's fascination with the space program had diminished. The major TV networks did not even carry the broadcast. Nine minutes after it was over, disaster struck.

Oxygen tank No. 2 blew up, causing tank No. 1 to fail also. The normal supply of electricity, light, and water was lost. And the crew was over 200,000 miles (321,800 kilometers) from earth. They did not even have enough power to turn the craft around and head back home. Thirteen minutes after the explosion, Lovell looked out the window of the CSM *Odyssey* and saw clouds of oxygen spewing from the craft into the black hole of space.

After one hour of frantic communications with Mission Control, it was decided that the astronauts would use the LM as a "lifeboat." There were no procedures or manuals for the situation. Years of grueling training had not prepared the astronauts and Mission Control for such an emergency. New procedures had to be tested on the ground in simulators, then passed up to the men in space.

With only 15 minutes of power left, the astronauts went into the LM *Aquarius*. The LM was built for only 45 hours of use. The men had to stretch it to 90 hours. Luckily there was enough oxygen. But the LM was designed to support two men for two days. Now it would have to support three men over four days.

The astronauts had to turn off every electrical device—including the flight computers—to have enough power to return home. Water was the real problem. It was needed to cool the craft on the return to earth. The astronauts were rationed to just 6 ounces (177 milliliters) of water a day—one-fifth of the normal amount. The food that needed to be mixed with water could not be eaten.

The men could have died from the exhaust of their own lungs. When a person breathes, he or she inhales oxygen and exhales carbon dioxide, which is poisonous in large amounts. The canisters that scrubbed the carbon dioxide from the air of the LM were filling up fast. Using plastic bags, cardboard, and tape, the astronauts rigged scrubbers to clean the air.

The temperature in the LM dropped to near freezing. The astronauts spent days in the dim light shivering.

The new flight plan was to let *Apollo 13* circle the moon once. Then, when the module came around the other side of the moon, the circling action would "throw" the craft towards earth. Even in their terrible situation, the men took time to study the moon as they flew high above it. It was still an awe-inspiring sight.

After the lunar orbit, the astronauts had to make a "course correction" to align the spacecraft to return to earth. This meant firing up the engines on the *Aquarius*. Without the computers to guide them, the crew used the sun as a guidepost and fired the engines. If they made the wrong calculations, they would bounce off the earth's atmosphere and be lost in space. With luck and skill they realigned the craft properly. *Apollo 13* was on its way home.

Five hours before *Apollo 13* was to land, the astronauts crawled back into the cold, clammy *Odyssey*. It had to be powered up with the last remaining energy so the computer could guide the astronauts home. Everything was damp, and the astronauts were afraid of an explosion from the wet panels. Luckily, safeguards had been built against sparks after the *Apollo 1* fire.

Four hours before landing, the astronauts shed the damaged service module. For the first time they could see what had happened as it floated away in space. "There's one whole side of that spacecraft missing," said Lovell. Now the crew worried that the heat shield on their module might be damaged. Temperatures reached up to 4,000 degrees Fahrenheit during reentry.

Three hour later, the men parted with their lifeboat *Aquarius*. There was a tense, four-minute radio blackout when the crew was streaking through the atmosphere. Mission Control thought the men had burned up on reentry. Then the three orange and white parachutes holding the command module popped onto the TV screens. The crew had landed safely!

Over one billion people on earth had followed the drama on TV. A cheer went up across the world when the astronauts crawled out of their cabin as it floated on the warm South Pacific Ocean.

In 1995, a movie called *Apollo 13* starring Tom Hanks portrayed the flight of the unlucky *Odyssey*.

THE LAST LANDINGS

Apollo 14 successfully landed in the moon's Fra Mauro region. Astronauts Alan Shepard and Commander Edgar D. Mitchell spent 9 hours outside the LM *Antares* collecting 98 pounds (44 kilograms) of rocks. They set up the ALSEP and a laser mirror while Major Stuart A. Roosa circled the moon in the CSM *Kitty Hawk.* TV watchers on earth laughed as Shepard drove a golf ball one-handed across the moon's surface.

Apollo 15 was targeted to the Hadley Apennine Mountains. The flight lasted from July 26 to August 7, 1971. Colonel David R. Scott and Lieutenant Colonel James B. Irwin landed the LM *Falcon,* while Major Alfred M. Worden circled overhead in the CSM *Endeavor.* This mission included a Lunar Roving Vehicle (LRV), which was a battery-powered "jeep" that could carry the astronauts across the moon.

Scott and Irwin explored the mountain slopes for a total of 18 hours, 36 minutes. They collected 173 pounds (78 kilograms) of soil and rock samples. The men explored a deep gorge called the Hadley Rille, but it was too steep to climb. Worden took thousands of photographic maps of the moon. After driving the Lunar Rover 7 miles (11.2 kilometers), Scott and Irwin set up another ALSEP. After a successful mission, the astronauts returned to earth.

Right: Astronaut David Scott of *Apollo 15* prepares to drive the Lunar Rover.

The *Apollo 16* mission lasted from April 16-27, 1972. Commander John Young and Charles Duke landed the LM *Orion* on the Descartes Highlands. Lieutenant Commander Ken Mattingly II orbited the moon in the CSM *Casper.* Young and Duke spent 20 hours, 14 minutes outside the LM and collected 210 pounds (95 kilograms) of rocks and soil.

The astronauts set up ultra-violet cameras for astronomical observations. They took deep core rock samples. Several other experiments were also performed.

Launched on December 7, 1972, *Apollo 17* was the final manned mission to the moon. Harrison H. Schmitt, a professional scientist, was sent on this flight. He landed in the LM *Challenger* with Eugene Cernan. They spent 22 hours on the moon. Overhead in the CSM *America* was Lieutenant Commander Ronald Evans. The crew returned to earth on December 19, 1972.

Below: Astronaut David Scott sits on the lunar rover waiting for his partner, James Irwin.

END OF APOLLO

The Apollo moon landings were a great scientific achievement. Over 1,000 pounds (453 kilograms) of lunar rock and soil were taken from 2,000 different sights on the moon. In addition, the missions left instruments to measure lunar gravity, magnetism, solar radiation, and more.

The Apollo astronauts were the smartest and bravest explorers in history. They helped unravel the moon's origins. They discovered the moon to be made of volcanic basalt dating from the birth of the solar system—4.6 billion years ago.

After six moon landings in four years, America seemed to lose interest. The projects were too expensive. The next step, a manned flight to Mars, would cost billions. The money wasn't there. Bold plans for manned space stations were cut back. NASA developed less expensive plans like the Space Shuttles—large winged aircraft that could be flown into orbit and returned to earth to be used again. The Apollo missions regularly flew 240,000 miles (386,160 kilometers) away from earth. The Space Shuttle would fly 240 miles (386 kilometers) into space.

The world had changed since President Kennedy called America to the moon. But for a brief four years, America put its best foot forward into space. The daring vision of a people acted itself out in a high drama across the skies of outer space. Like the Greek god himself, the astronauts of Project Apollo rode their flaming chariots across the sky.

GLOSSARY

astronaut

A person who is trained for spaceflight. From the Latin words "star traveler."

Cape Canaveral

A place on the Atlantic side of Florida where missiles and rockets are launched. Most missions into outer space were launched from Cape Canaveral.

CSM (combined command and service module)

A space vehicle that held both the flight controls and the mechanical equipment used for a moonlanding. The CSM carried the astronauts to the moon and back to earth.

escape velocity

The speed a spacecraft needs to travel in order to escape the gravitational pull of the earth.

liftoff

Start of a rocket's flight from its launch pad, also called "blastoff."

NASA

National Aeronautics and Space Administration. The United States government agency formed in 1958 to research and launch satellites and spacecraft.

quarantine

A strict isolation to prevent the spread of disease.

splashdown

The landing of a space vehicle in the ocean.

sub-orbital

A flight into space that does not involve traveling around the earth in orbit.

thruster

A rocket engine that propels a spacecraft.

tranquility

Peace. The first lunar landing was at a place called the Sea of Tranquility.

BIBLIOGRAPHY

Aldrin, Buzz. *Men From Earth*. New York: Bantam Books, 1989.

Arco Publishing. *Out of This World.* New York: Arco Publishing, 1985.

Cortright, Edgar M, editor. *Apollo Expeditions to the Moon.* Washington, D.C.: NASA, 1975.

Dolan, Edward F. *Famous Firsts in Space*. New York: Cobblehill Books, 1989.

Gatland, Kenneth. *The Illustrated Encyclopedia of Space Technology*. New York: Orion Books, 1989.

Kennedy, Gregory P. *The First Men in Space*. New York: Chelsea House Publishers, 1991.

Olney, Ross Robert. *American in Space*. New York: Thomas Nelson, Inc., 1970.

Pogue, William R. *How Do You Go To The Bathroom In Space?* New York: Tom Doherty Books, 1985.

INDEX